Telling It Like It Is

fairytales and personal truth

Nick Owen

Telling it like it is

Transitions publications
Oxford

www.trans-itions.com

First published in 2004 by Transitions Publications 8 Market St, Charlbury
Oxon OX7 3PN

Transitions Publications

Transitions publications is concerned with bringing to the public cutting
edge ideas in areas of psycho-social and emotional education.

Fields covered include psychology, psychotherapy, literature, drama,
personal and social development, poetry and photography.

For more information: info@trans-itions.com or visit www.trans-itions.com

Tel 01608 811746

Nick Owen
Telling it like it is
ISBN 0-9547390-0-0

"One should only read books which bite and sting one.

If a book we are reading does not wake us up...

what is the point of reading?

A book must be the axe which smashes

the frozen sea within us." Kafka.

Dedication

To my daughters Holly and Rosie,
the truth at the heart of my fairytales

and to Leonie Bennett,
whose passion drew them out of me.

Acknowledgements

I wish to thank The Playspace Trust for helping me begin this work, and Westminster Pastoral Foundation and the Oxford Centre for Human Relations for supporting its development over many years. Closer to home, I want to thank my editor, Gillian Darwent, without whom it might never have come to print, and my teachers, colleagues and students. I particularly want to mention David Holt and Alida Gersie, from the early years, and Mary Duhig and Marie-Carmen Mendez, from more recent times. Most recently I want to thank Charlbury School children for being my test bed. Borders in Oxford and the Shed in Charlbury have provided welcome public venues for my first public performances. Special thanks to Rob and Ed who have encouraged me to go ahead with publication, and to Elizabeth, Jane, Tony, Clare, and Jenifer, who listened and encouraged so warmly.

CONTENTS

Introduction by the author

The Tales

Beauty and the Beast
Cinderella
The Frog Prince
Hanzel and Gretel
Little Red Riding Hood
Rapunzel
Sleeping Beauty
Jack and the Bean-stalk
The Ice Queen
Goldilocks
Snow White

Applications for learning;

1) Personal development workshops

2) Courses and entertainment for businesses and organisation development

3) Schools and colleges

4) Professional development for those who work with young people

Introduction by the author

In working with fairy tales as a therapist and teacher for over thirty years, I have found that they tell the fundamental truths of growing up, a universal story. Fairy tales describe basic patterns in our life-stories. Reviewing them can have a strong impact on our inner worlds. This book explores the most popular and formative tales, as chosen for enactment and analysis in personal development workshops. Many adults have told me the stories they recall from childhood and reached back through them in to their personal experiences of the trials of youth. I have found that the relationship patterns in these tales influence perceptions, choices, and possibilities for personal development or even transformation in profound and surprising ways.

Therapy has often been described as a project of creating a satisfactory biography. I believe that a key to maturation and personal growth is a revaluation of the stories we learned in childhood. In reviewing a fairy tale as an older person we can cultivate a vision that nurtures our best qualities. The central tasks of the characters in these stories include finding authenticity, being loyal to cherished values, and having compassion towards oneself and others. Integration involves a willingness to come to terms with our stories as they are, and what they have the potential to become.

"Telling it like it is," takes best loved tales and weaves them into humourous verses that maintain the fundamental structure of the old stories, while placing them into life situations of the children and parents of twenty first century Britain. It draws on many years experience of therapeutic work with children and families. The reader is invited to examine how awareness of psychological narratives may reveal their overlooked options and hidden inner strengths. Through rewriting the tales as about modern lives, modern children, modern parents, I hope to connect you with the thrill of searching for your own personal myth, and a clear sense of life-purpose.

I have attempted to give back to these stories the relevance to real lives and real children of today that a stream of emasculated publications for an idealised nursery may have taken away. A later publication, "Journeys to integration," will look at how hidden motivations and expectations shape the unfolding adventure both in the story and in our lives. There I will examine how personal storylines can be revised over time.

This is not a book for very young children. These stories tell the truth of life, not a rose-tinted version of it. They are funny and outrageous, full of threats and anxiety, fear and anger, success and failure, despair and triumph. They engage head-on with the sex and the violence of the modern world. Rather than hiding or sentimentalizing human problems I have told it as it really is for many children whose families have fallen on hard times. The children in them are the kind of children who ring child-line by the thousand each year. The book gives them a voice. It tells their stories. While little red riding-hood is sexually precocious, Hanzel and Gretel are lured towards child prostitution. Cinderella is a drug addict. The Ice Queen is an avaricious research doctor, experimenting on children. Jack's bean-stalk is an internet phone. It is a needle from a syringe that knocks out Sleeping Beauty. The Frog Prince is a victim of child abuse. Beauty's beast is a time-share salesman. So it goes on.

Don't buy this book if you need the safety of symbols projected onto distant times and far away places. Do buy it if you want to be grabbed by the intensity and power of the fairy tale as retold for the modern world. The children in these stories are heroic. They face very serious problems, make big decisions and come through victorious. By the end they have really grown up.

Some or all of them will touch your own sore spots and show you new ways forward, if you are brave enough. They will make you laugh and they will make you cry. Use them for entertainment, for self renewal, for educational, personal and social development work.

At the back of the book I offer suggestions for their use in schools, colleges, personal development workshops and management development.

I recommend them. They are at the heart of my life's work.

Nick Owen: January 2004

BEAUTY AND THE BEAST

Come, daughter dear, we'll have a feast,
The tale of beauty and her beast.

It starts one dark December day
With bills that father could not pay.
His wife is gone, his daughters three
Are home with him, watching T.V.

A lovely mansion, once they had,
Before his businesses went bad.

A cottage now is what they rent,
'Cos all Dad's money has been spent.

The older daughters, tall and strong,
Are sure their father's in the wrong.

They fear that soon they'll have to work
Or marry to some awful jerk,
Who doesn't care that father's poor
And sure to be an utter bore.

The youngest girl, still cute and pretty,
Just a bit like Walter Mitty,
Doesn't care for wealth or riches,
Thinks her sisters both are bitches.

Thinks her father is just great,
Sisters are the ones to hate,
Cleans the house from dawn till night,
Wants to put the whole thing right.

Daddy opens up a letter,
Thinks it's work, so he had better
Grab his hat and coat and boots,
Pack his very finest suits,
Head off through the blustery gales,
With all his mind on one thing, sales.

Full of hope he asks his girls,
What to bring to dress their curls,
Should the business come his way,
And brighten up their winters day.

The older girls want silver, gold
And diamonds, for they'd been told
That diamonds will last forever,
While other pleasures simply never
Last.

Beauty wasn't bothered much
With lasting treasures she could clutch.
She asked her dad, "Do you suppose,
That you could bring me back a rose."

Dad revved the car and drove away,
To get there for the end of day,
But in his hurry lost his way,
Missed a turn on the motorway.

Night descended, down came snow.
His progress now was very slow.
A roadside ad said, "bring your mum,
And view our condominium"

He ventured in, for he was tired,
Parked the car that he had hired,
Found a room and went to sleep,
Hoping that it would be cheap.

Morning came and breakfast too,
They even made a splendid brew.
But nowhere could he find a bill,
Nor waiters, not one ringing till.

The garden there was full of roses.
He wondered "Who would you suppose is
In charge here.
It's mighty queer,
A place to work and rest and play
And not to have a bill to pay.

In the gardens, he took a stroll,
Feeling he was on a roll.
He picked a very pretty rose,
Whose scent had so impressed his nose.

"That seals the deal", a voice boomed out
From something looking like a snout,
On such a very ugly head
That daddy fainted, banged his head.

On waking, beast-man made it plain,
His life was forfeit, down the drain.
He'd stay in prison here forever
The price was one that he could never
Pay.

Unless he made another trade,
A bargain for his daughter made.
If she could come here in his stead,
To keep his house and make his bed.

Now Dad was in a lot of trouble.
Life felt like a heap of rubble.
He wanted just to save his life,
To get away from beastly strife.

To live a free man one more day,
He'd even give his girls away.
And so he hurried home to see
If one of them might just agree.

The condominium looked fine.
He hoped she would adjust in time,
To living there among the roses,
Avoiding men with ugly noses.

The older girls would not agree.
They said "You can't do that to me."
But Beauty loved her dear old dad,
And maybe just a little mad,

She quickly set off in his place,
With shining eyes and gentle grace,
To find the condominium.
Free food and drink to fill her tum.

The beast, she did not think of much,
If she could just evade his touch.
If she avoided wearing glasses,
She might not even see his passes.

She didn't fear sex in the back of his carriage.
Sure, hadn't he asked for her hand in marriage!
To this she simply would never agree.
The man was as ugly as ugly could be.

It certainly was a big beautiful place.
She'd have liked the beast too, if it weren't for his face.
The longer she stayed,
The more that they played.
He flattered her,
Sang to her,
And his love he displayed.

Then one day he gave her an internet phone,
The sort you make ring for you any old tone.
She calls her old man,
Just as fast as she can.

He's ill, she must go to him,
Fearing beast's ban.

But the beast is compassionate, says she can go.
He bids her remember him, here in the snow.

Soon our beauty is home, where she settles right in.
Her father recovers, once he's off the gin.
Even her sisters are glad that she's back.
Without her the cleaning had gone very slack.

And Beauty forgets about beast in the snow,
And her promise, that back to him soon she would go.
Daddy is happily tucked up in bed,
While beast is alone wishing that he was dead.

Forsaken by Beauty, he is fading away,
While Beauty and family start to go gay.
Beast's big furry coat has gone suddenly grey.

The phone rings for Beauty, and to her dismay
If she doesn't come now he may die, today!

Beauty is touched by her beast's awful plight.
She puts on her coat and sets off in the night.
She prays when she gets there he may be all right,
But when she arrives she's appalled by the sight

Of the dying away of the man in the beast.
Was he any more ugly, no, not in the least.

But he lay nearly dead,
Half asleep on the bed.
And vastly to the girl's surprise,
She wished they had been wed.

Mysteriously, as if from above,
Our heroine has fallen in love.

Soon her tears begin to flow,
As all her love and sadness show.

She stoops to kiss his shaggy head,
As he lays suffering on the bed.
Her tear drops fall upon his snout,
Which opens all the magic out.

And so before our very eyes,
The beast escapes from his disguise.
The ugliness has all turned pretty,
A very strange effect of pity.

The man from out the beast emerges,
And joy within her heart it surges.
The snout has turned into a nose.
He stands and strikes a handsome pose.

He finally begins to speak.
His voice has gone a little weak.
"It was greed that made a beast of me.
My punishment you all could see.

But if I could love and not be needy,
Desire you, but not get seedy,
Then maybe I'd inspire your love,
Be rescued by the Gods above.

And so at last my heart is full.
I'm finished with this load of bull.
I'll sell these time-shares never more.
They made me such a dreadful bore.
Now thanks to you I'm out the door."

So finally our couple wed.
The honeymoon was in the med.

Well, daughter dear,
My tale is told.
You will grow up, while I grow old.

The beasts will come to look at you,
And you'll be glad you always knew,
With love, and tear drops, and a little yeast,
You can bring culture to your chosen beast.

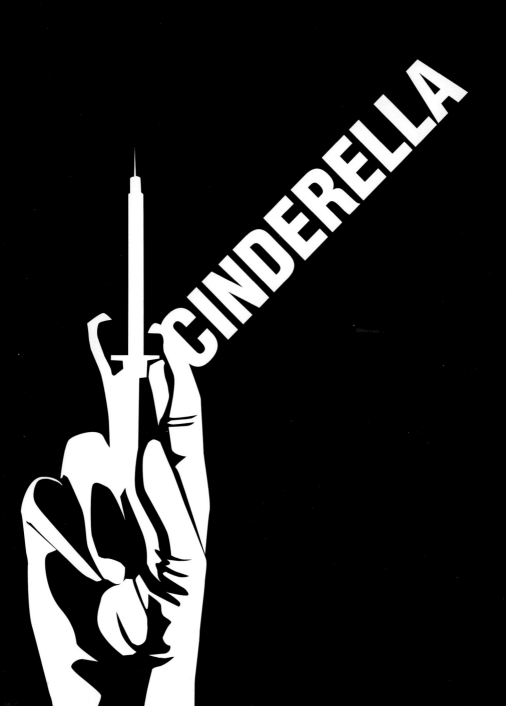

CINDERELLA

Come close, my dear, and listen to
The tale of Cinderella.
You know, the one got married to
That super princely fella.

They called her Cinders, because she
Kept sleeping in the ashes.
This was her way of keeping warm
And dodging step-mum's lashes.

Her father was very far from kind.
Her mother's death he did not mind.
There was no grieving on his part.
Her mother died of a broken heart.

He married step mum much too quick,
Which left young Sindy feeling sick.
Inheriting two ugly sisters,
Who liked to cover her in blisters.

Now Jessabelle worshiped Judy and Jill,
Her girls by an earlier marriage.
Sindy, she would have been happy to kill,
And dump in the refuse carriage.

Her children they just loved to tease her.
Step mum vowed that she wouldn't please her.
Father did not seem to care,
And mostly he just was not there.

He had not really loved her mother,
But step-mum thrilled him like no other.
Sindy, he too left broken hearted,
Grieving for her dear departed.

She went to sit among the graves,
While sisters spent their time at raves.
Sindy dressed in shabby jeans,
Was fed on toast and cold baked beans.

But Sindy had a lovely face
And had her mother's quiet grace.
While sisters both had ugly faces,
With all their bits in the oddest places.
Sindy's figure was just like a Barbie.
Theirs were suited much more for the army.

The sisters were extremely jealous
Of her attraction for the fellas.
But Sindy did not seem to care
Boys might as well have not been there.

Her dad turned slowly into a loser,
Spending his time, more and more at the boozer.

The girls beat Sindy black and blue,
And stuffed her sweet head down the loo.
Their mother was happy to join right in,
Kicking the girl, with a hideous grin.

Sindy was soon in deep despair.
She cut off her locks of golden hair,
And to the grave yard she'd repair,
To stick a needle in her arm,
Which did some good, but much more harm,
And no one cared, or gave the alarm.

She stole from shops to pay the dealer,
Who liked to think of herself as a healer,
With remedies for every ill.
A pity that they sometimes kill!

She'd sit there under the graveyard tree,
The tracks on her veins for all to see.
Dad was getting increasingly vexed
With Jessabelle, just sex obsessed.

Seeing Sindy so depressed,
The dealer vowed to do her best,
In shifting guilt from off her chest,
Lends Sindy clothes and shoes and make-up,
Trying to postpone her break up.
She lifts her up from mother's grave.

Says, "Sindy, you shall go to the rave!
Now take this tab of ecxtacy
And also this, its LSD. "

She bundles Sindy into her car
And drives her there. It isn't far.

Inside our heroine hides in a corner,
Discussing the scene with a friend called Lorna.
But the dealer had also forgotten to warn her,
The drugs would start to wear off around midnight.
She had better leave then, if she wanted to stay right.

On centre stage was a wonderful dancer,
A man who seemed to have every answer.
This was a man who was certainly regal,
Though his blood wasn't blue, and his title not legal,
On the dancing floor he just soared like an eagle.

He wasn't the artist who used to be Prince,
Though the fans called him Gary, his mum called him Vince.
Every girl there had his light in their eyes,
And everyone thought him a prince among guys.

Sindy looks round, and to her great surprise,
All of the fear in her suddenly dies.
She was not a girl who thought much about men,
But when she saw this one she turned on, and then,
It was though she was meeting the man of her dreams,
The sort with those wonderful sexual themes.

She leaps to her feet and jumps out on the floor.
Suddenly Sindy's in touch with her core.

She can dance from her spirit and dance from her soul,
And dance with her body beyond her control,
And yet she unerringly makes for her goal.

Our heroine, inspired by love,
Is dancing like a turtle dove.

Our hero, (the man who looks just like a prince)
Starts gazing at her from his coffee and mints.
It's nothing to do with his family tree,
The man is a modern style cel-eb-rit-y.
He knows what he wants and it has to be she.

This is the very best rave of the year.
The sisters, of course, simply have to be here,
Either snorting cocaine, or just swilling their beer.

They ask if its Sindy out there on the floor.
It's surely not possible, she's such a bore!

The lovers dance like Posh and Beckham.
There's nothing in the world can wreck'em.
But finally, just when he's holding her near,
Our heroine suddenly starts to feel queer.
She slips from her jacket and makes for the door,
Just when the audience's screaming for more.

Our hero's left standing there, holding her jacket.
Deep in the lining he finds a small packet.
The dealer's left her phone in there.
He hugs it like a teddy bear.

He vows to ring up every number,
And til its done he will not slumber.

He swears to wed the girl with the phone,
And until then he'll sleep alone,
Which isn't a virtue for which he was known.
No one could count all the seed he had sown!

His fam'ly and friends said he must have been pissed.
But it was her beautiful dancing he missed.
Like the music of Mozart, the playing of Liszt,
And all for a girl he had not even kissed,
Her dancing so special he cannot resist.

The memory bank holds at least fifty names,
So the hero has little time left to play games.

Garry goes visiting all of these girls.
Some are the daughters of Barons and Earls.
Our hero, he asks to see all of their dances,
Which quickly is bringing an end to their chances.

At last he gets to Sindy's house.
He asks to meet her mother's spouse.

While Gary is trying to talk with him,
Poor Sindy's sent to uncle Jim.
With Sindy, so carefully out of the way,
The step-mother sees her girls winning the day.

Judy starts to show her dance,
But he retreats at her advance.
He sits and watches for a while.
Her best can't even make him smile.

Jill has yet more determination.
She dances way beyond her station.
She strips and dances in his lap.
She thinks he is a lucky chap.
Though, even if she dances well,
He can't abide her armpit smell.

Garry exits in despair.
He'd hoped to find the answer there.
He wanders slowly down the street,
Staring sadly at his feet.

Sindy sees him passing there,
And wonders if she might just dare
To talk to him.

To Sindy its just infra-dig
Admitting that she wore a wig.

No longer wearing pretty clothes,
She thinks, I really don't suppose
He'll recognise me in the street,
Unless of course, I use my feet.

The two are very quickly dancing
Its better than the best romancing.
Their feet, they hardly touch the ground,
To music played without a sound,
As both go spinning round and round.

They dance until they reach his car,
(The most expensive Jaguar.)
Both laughing as they drive away,
They start to plan their wedding day.

Well, daughter dear, my tale is done.
Much better now than when begun.
The lovers very soon are wed
And honeymooning in the Med.
Our Sindy's no more time for grieving,
She's concentrating on conceiving.

Is there a moral to this tale?
If you think hard, you will not fail.
Success comes when you find your bliss
And dancing's where the answer is.
It isn't really in his kiss.

THE FROG PRINCE

THE FROG PRINCE

Lesley was a young Princess.
Not of Royal blood, I guess.
But Daddy was the king of news,
An anchor man with his own views.
It earned him kingly revenues.

Their home looked like some ancient tower
And represented daddy's power.
The garden too was very splendid.
With great high walls it was defended.
These kept out the paparazzi
So none of them were saying, "grazi".

But Lesley had to play alone
Or call friends on the telephone.

She liked to play with golden balls
And romp around in overalls.
She often threw them in the air
And tried to catch them as a pair.

Now one day a precious ball fell in the water.
Her dad, much too busy to search for his daughter.
She sat beside the pond and cried.
T'was not as though she had not tried.
The ball had vanished deep inside.

Then out of Daddy's water feature,
Emerged a green and slimy creature.
Not a lizard or a newt,
(Some famous people find those cute).
Addressing her upon a log
Was an amazing talking frog.

He offered her a special deal.
I promise you that this is real!

He'd go dive and fetch her ball.
It would not take him long at at all.
Then she would take him in her house
And love him just like her pet mouse.

In fact, to love him rather better.
He wrote it in a slimy letter.
He must dine upon her table,
And share her food, if he was able.

Then afterwards to share her bed,
With little pillows for his head.

Now Lesley, she really just wanted her ball.
She hardly considered this froggy at all.
Preposterous to keep a deal
With a talking frog. Come on. Get real!

The frog disappeared and came back with her toy.
She cared not if this were a girl or a boy.
She ran away, back to her house,
Which made our froggy grouse and grouse.

"You promised you would take me too.
Now what am I supposed to do?"
Slowly he hopped up to her door,
Requesting honouring his score.
To Lesley this was just a bore.

How could any frog expect
A human child to show respect?
Frogs are meant for vivisection.
She'd done it at her school inspection.

But dad has heard the froggy croak.
He does not find it just a joke.
For he'd done a programme on animal rights,
And knew of the animal terrorists' fights.

"Now, Lesley, let this frog come in.
No, you can't put him in the bin.
I'm not risking bombs being thrown at my home.
You must understand he's a frog, not a gnome.

If you agreed to make this deal,
Then froggy has to share your meal.
And he will have to share your bed,
If that is truly what you said.

So froggy got to share her plate.
Her food, which once had tasted great,
Had suddenly lost all its flavour.
For frog it was a meal to savour.

But how's a girl that's so well bred
To take a slimy frog to bed?

She has to take him to her room.
She wants to crush him with a broom.

But daddy says that he must stay.
Poor Lesley can't throw him away.

The two of them get into bed.
Its not as if the pair are wed.
She puts a bolster in between.
Do you think that this girl is mean?

But frog insists he sleep on her pillow
Or, he declares, her father will know.

To Lesley, that's the final straw.
She hurls the frog against the door.

The froggy makes a dreadful squelch.
Lesley lets out a satisfied belch.

But what is this upon the floor?
Its dark inside, so she's not sure.
Its much too big to be a frog.
Our Lesley's suddenly agog.

The frog's become a sexy male.
He pulls himself up on the rail.
"I guess," he says, " We need a chat"
But that's not really where she's at.

Talking with frogs is bad enough,
But talk with men, that's really rough!
She pulls the stranger into bed.
The man is happy to be led.

She reckons that her dad's agreed,
And so the two begin to breed.

Next day he takes the girl away.
He has a place where they can stay.

A witch had put a spell on him,
A relative called Uncle Jim.
His world was covered up with slime.
He hoped he'd be released in time.

If any girl would honour him,
But not for all his features grim.

She'd had to get into a lather
To find she could oppose her father.

And now at last our tale is ended
And all of this abuse is mended.

At least, that is the way I see it
Unless, of course, you don't agree it.

HANZEL AND GRETEL

Come close, my children, sit with me.
You've heard this at your mother's knee.
The tale of Hanzel and his sister Gretel,
And tests which put them on their mettle.

The forest where they lived has gone.
The sawyer's work is more than done.
Though woods are saved by conservation,
In this and every western nation.

Our modern jungle is the city.
These places, which are not so pretty,
Are often hard and cruel and gritty,
With very little room for pity.

Our modern heroes, Dick and Jane
Were driven very near insane,
Escaping from a cruel life,
The victims of their dad's new wife.

Their mum had left them with their dad,
A man who was not all that bad.
But he married a woman, a bit of a witch,
Who was, for the children, a terrible bitch.

She'd lock them in their rooms at night,
Then she and dad would have a fight.
The kids, she treated very hard.
She fed them just on bread and lard.

She thought it fun to box their ears,
While clucking, "You're such little dears."
Her parenting, so inconsistent,
To any care they got resistant.

One night they heard their parents say,
The children were just in the way.
They would be better off "in care"
So they had better send them there.

The kids had seen some films on care.
They knew they'd not be happy there.
Care homes were places full of abuses.
It's time to escape, with no excuses.

The door is locked, so out the window,
Is how our very daring twins go.

They both dash off to catch the bus,
Without one little shred of fuss.

But then they find they have no money.
The driver says," Get off now, sonny."

They have to hitch a lift instead.
Much safer to have stayed in bed.

A lorry stops, they both get in.
The engine makes a dreadful din.
They might have had a chance to win,
If they had found some other kin,

But Dick and Jane had no relations
In this or any other nations.
The two of them were forced to go
To some place that they did not know.

The driver took them from the coast,
To the city that they'd heard of most.
We're told some streets are paved with gold.
Before you find them you'll grow old

In London town, up the West End,
You think the lights will be your friend.
The neon shines so very bright,
But casts deep shadows through the night,
Exaggerates the children's plight.

Their only shelter, Hungerford bridge,
Was more like sleeping in a fridge.

Driven by hunger, pain and fears,
The children soon break down in tears.

Then suddenly their cries are heard.
They're spotted by a pretty bird.
She flutters down to them to say,
She knows a place where they can stay.

She's dressed in very gaudy feathers,
Stuff like lace and different leathers.
Jane admires these sexy clothes,
Says she, "I fancy some of those."

Though Dick agrees that she's a looker,
He thinks this bird could be a hooker.

But children, hungry, tired and cold,
They follow her into her fold.

A narrow lane in old Soho,
Is where our children have to go.

A house that's full of pretty clothes,
That barely cover, and expose
All sorts of things, below and above.
The sort of clothes for making love.

Emporium of earthly delights,
A shop to spice up adults' nights,
But not protecting childrens' rights.

A woman, who has silver hair,
Explains that she's the mistress there.
Though she is old and none too pretty,
She says to call her aunty Kitty.

Upstairs there is a place to stay,
As long as they stay out the way.,
She'll even let Jane have some clothes,
Such very pretty panty-hose.

The tired children go to sleep,
Not sure what company they keep.

The woman seems so very kind,
But trusting makes the children blind.

They wake to find that they are caught,
Their bid for freedom all for naught.
The children find that they are slaves.
They threaten them with early graves.

And no one knows that they are there
In Soho, why would someone care?

At night they're kept inside a cage.
It does not matter how they rage.

They're hidden very far from view
And quite unknown to me and you.

Before long, they start hitting Dick.
They frighten Jane. It makes her sick.

The captors soon have all the aces.
Its written in the children's faces.

Jane must do whatever they say,
If Dick's to see another day.

She'll have to work in a place like an oven,
The den of all this evil coven.

At night the children get more plucky.
They make a plan. They might get lucky.

The woman's getting old and frail,
Perhaps she'll get them out of gaol.
They'll try to catch her in a trick,
Pretend that they are feeling sick.

The woman with the silver hair,
Comes shuffling up to see the pair.
Jane has to see some men tonight,
And do some things which just aren't right.

She takes Jane to the coven door,
But then she's tripped and hits the floor.
Jane bangs her head with an iron claw.

She strikes again upon her head,
To make sure that the witch is dead.

She finds the key for Dick's release,
But they don't dare to tell the police.

Instead the two of them have crept
To find where all the money's kept.
The money's hid inside a vault,
Where they took Dick for his assault.

There really is a lot of cash
Inside this place. They make a stash.

Just now they feel extremely glad
To go back home and see their dad.

But first the two must separate,
To dodge the wicked men they hate.

One of them holds all the cash.
The other has to make a dash.

While Jane is safe across the river,
Dick stabs a bad guy in the liver.

They did not make an idle boast.
They both get safely to the coast,
Where dad and step-mum had such fights,
That he had punched out both her lights.

Defeated, she had gone away
To find some other bloke to play.

To see his kids, dad was delighted.
Now most of all their wrongs were righted,

Especially now they all were rich,
Their lives went on without a hitch.

Well, children, now my tale is done.
Go out and play, and have some fun.
But first, my darlings, tell me true,

What were these children meant to do?
Please know, before I hear your voices,
That life's determined by your choices.

NOT SO LITTLE RED RIDING HOOD

Come, sit with me, my daughter dear.
We shall be warm and comfy here.
To hear a tale that's old and strong.
It shouldn't really take that long
To tell.
The telling is a magic spell.

Our heroine is growing tall
Though mum and dad think she's still small.
She's seen it all on television,
Wants to start her own incision.

She's cutting her own mark in life,
Though far too young to be a wife.

Her parents call her little Kay,
As pretty as the buds in May,
With emerald eyes and raven hair.
She's made some older people stare.

For winning smiles you couldn't beat her,
And some folk called her young Lolita.

But she was known throughout the town
For dressing up, not dressing down,
And most of all for her cycle helmet,
Bright scarlet with a long red pelmet.

Flashing here and flashing there,
She gave old people quite a scare.
She really had a super bike.
They called her every kind of tyke.

Then one day mum called home from work,
In dreary weather full of murk,
Explaining, grandma was suffering ills,
And Kay had better ride round with her pills.

Now grandma lived on the council estate,
And she'd better get going before it got late.
Mum says its a bit of a jungle round there,
So being out late could give Kay quite a scare.

But with all those lovely shops on the way,
Our heroine risked just a little delay.

Such lovely dresses and sexy new tops,
Hardly surprising our heroine stops.

Frederic Wolf was an uncle of hers,
And he wasn't one of those mangy old curs,
But a very smart man, decked out in his best,
Though down underneath
He still wears a string vest.

The man sees her standing outside the boutique,
And Freddie, who's really a bit of a freak,
Accosts her, but in a such a friendly way,
Sartorial, elegant, ever so gay.

She tells him she's off to her grandmother's place.
Our Freddie decides on a bit of a race.

He jumps in his Probe and he's there in a tick,
His lips round his teeth he's beginning to lick.
Grandma's dispatched with just one little prick
With a needle, he says, will stop her feeling sick.

The body is easily hid in the shed,
So Freddie can wrap himself up in her bed.
But surely our girl's not so easily led.

The scene now is set there, for her entrapment.
At least I am pretty sure that's what the chap meant.
For Freddie Wolf's mind is just horribly bent.
He covers his body in grandmama's scent.

Soon, our heroine comes on the scene,
Looking just like love's young dream.
She throws herself in grandma's lap.
My goodness, what a lucky chap.

"Grandma, you have such big eyes.
They really are a nice surprise"
Says Kay,
"Lets play."

"Oh Darling, I am feeling ill.
I'd better pop another pill."
Says Fred,
Still hiding in the bed.

"Grandma you have the roughest hair,"
She says,
As she's stroking him,
Here and there.

Freddie, by now, is very excited.
It's just as if he had been invited.

"Why, Granny, you have such sensuous lips,"
Says Kay, with a casual swish of her hips.

Poor Freddie is going a little bit wild,
But as Grandma, he thinks that he has to stay mild.
"They're so good for sucking things, my little child."

"Oh granny, your teeth are so shiny and hard,
You're just like the animals out in the yard."
For Freddy, this last is a little too much,
And something has simply gone wrong with his crutch.
"Oh Granny, I thought you were ever so butch."

Its now that the man from the council comes in.
He starts to drag grandmother off to the bin,
And Freddie is going to get done for his sin.

Then evil Fred goes all of a quiver
And throws his fat body right into the river.

Grandma wakes from a wonderful sleep,
And no one has heard any more of the creep,
Who threw himself into the river that day.
So either he died, or he got clean away.

And now my tale is nearly done.
Kay has cycled home to her mum.

She tells of evil older men,
Who tried to eat her up, and then
She easily got the better of them.

So, daughter dear,
My story's done.
It's time to go back to your mum.
And if this story has been pacey,
Its heroine a bit too racey,

Its the first time in a hundred years
That Riding Hood's not shedding tears!
And though the wolf always gets beaten,
It is the first where he's been eaten.
And bigger teeth you do not need,
To make a more successful breed.

RAPUNZEL (RAMPION)

Come listen, child, to this old tale,
In part, about the daring male,
But also about pregnancy,
A risky time for you or me.

A time when mum has special needs
To keep sustained her growing seeds.
And rampion was what Jill craved
To make sure that her babe was saved.

Her window showed the herb was growing
Right next door, by witch's sowing.
A weird old crone had put it there
And nurtured it with every care.

The sight of it just made Jill groan.
It made her sigh, it made her moan.
At last she told her husband Jack,
She begged him, could he bring some back?

But it was in the witch's garden,
He was afraid to beg her pardon.
The couple feared this witch's power.
They did not dare approach her tower.

Then Jill began to fade away,
She's getting weaker day by day.
Her craving's getting worse and worse.
She fears her child will never nurse.

"This stuff can save me and this child.
Without it I am going wild.
A desperation gnaws at me,
My darling, you must surely see
That rampion is all I crave.
Without it, we will share a grave,

All for the want of rampion.
Jack, won't you be my champion.
For rampion, oh rampion,
Please darling, be my champion"

Jack thinks his wife will maybe die,
The witch's garden he must try.

At dead of night he climbs the wall,
No signs of someone there at all,
He fills his arms with rampion
And hurries home, her champion.

So now his wife begins to feed
And for a while it meets her need,
But then, alas, there's not enough,
She has to have more of this stuff.

Jack must make his courage harden
Risk once more the witch's garden,
But this time, at the dead of night,
He can't escape the witch's might,

For she is waiting there for him.
She holds him with her visage grim.
She asks him what he's doing there.
These herbs are things she does not share.

Should she not punish this foul thief?
His fear has grown beyond belief.
Maybe she'll turn him to a toad
Or drag him off to her abode.

He told the witch about his wife
About his fearing for her life.
This rampion was what she needed.
With none, her future's much impeded.

The witch was moved with strange compassion,
She pondered it in her own fashion.
At last she offered Jack a deal
And wondered how the man might feel.

He'd save himself and his wife too
If this, he would agree to do.
The babe must go into her keeping,
(She'd make a spell to stop them weeping).

For this she'd spare the couples' lives.
If not, she'd cut them up with knives.

She gave him all her choicest greens,
Both magic herbs and runner beans,
To help the baby come out strong,
For now the birth would not be long.

His wife was struck down hard with grief
But she had to redeem her thief.
The babe was given to the witch.
The trade went through without a hitch.

The girl was taken to a tower,
Deep inside the witch's bower.
The child was in the forest hid,
Where no one saw the things she did.

"Rampion," she called the child.
The name was registered and filed.

The place in which the girl was kept,
In which she ate and drank and slept,
Was just beneath the rounded roof.
Against invasions, it was proof.

The spiral stair was hacked away.
The door was blocked up night and day.
The only way into her room,
Which must have seemed a second womb,
A little window in the wall,
An entrance fit for someone small.

The witch came round just once a day
And this is what she had to say,
"Rampion, please let down your hair.
For you, I've come along to care."

The girl lets down her long blonde hair.
The witch climbs up to join her there.
She visits every day at three
To cook the girl her special tea.

A Prince comes riding through the wood
For exercise. It did him good.
He hears the lovely Rampion's voice
And looks for her, since she's his choice.

But though he seeks, he cannot find,
For magic mystifies his mind,
Till one day when its nearly three
The witch, he happens there to see.

He sees her climb up Rampion's hair
And now he knows the answer's there.

He visits early in the morn,
Defying the old witch's scorn.

The couple don't have much to say.
They're busy with their lovers' play.

Till one day when the witch comes round
And Rampion lifts her from the ground,
She strangely gives the game away,
And this is what she had to say,

"Why is it when you look so small,
Your weight should be nothing at all?
I wonder how this can make sense,
You're so much heavier than my Prince."

Grizelda flies into a rage.
Our story's at a crucial stage.
She hatches up a nasty plan
To catch this unsuspecting man.

She snips right off poor Rampion's hair.
She banishes her from living there.
She's forced to wander far away
And find some dreadful place to stay.

She lets the hair down for the Prince.
She does not give out any hints.

He pulls himself up to her room
She screams, "This place should be your tomb."
With that she lets the tresses go.
He falls, and his descent's not slow,

And yet he does not reach the ground.
Into some thorns his body's bound.
He's overwhelmed by his surprise
And thorns have cut into his eyes.

The witch allows him to survive.
Though blind, the Prince can scarcely thrive.
For years he wanders through the wood
With nuts and berries for his food.

As years and years and years go by
He has much time to reason why
He found and then he lost his love,
His sight lost, tumbling from above.

He's built a lot of discipline,
Frustrated, but not giving in.

Then one day in the month of May
He hears some little children play.
He joins in playing with two twins.
It's here our happy end begins.

The twins are both our Rampion's boys
And they are both her pride and joys.
Then Rampion comes around to see
What on earth this noise could be.

But she is much distressed to find
Her lost love absolutely blind.
She feels so happy, yet so sad
To introduce them to their dad.

Her life, as single mum, is hard,
Keeping the pigs out in the yard,
But his has been just really rough.
At times, it has seemed all too tough.

Their heartache they cannot disguise
And nothing can hold back their cries.
She wipes her tears upon his eyes
And then, to both of their surprise,
His eyes are healed and he can see.
They're both as happy as can be.

The family travels to his home.
He needs a great big brush and comb
And fresh clothes, for their marriage feast.
She needs a wedding dress, at least.

The children are their parents' pages
And getting dressed-up takes them ages.
At last they have the ceremony,
Everybody finds it funny.

It's strange to end her simple life,
Becoming now a Prince's wife,
But all the hardships they had faced
Ensure that they are both well placed
To understand their people's plight
And sometimes they can put it right.

And now, my girl, this tale is ended.
If you endure, then pain gets mended.
If things go wrong, then don't just wail,
Keep going, and you will not fail.

SLEEPING BEAUTY

This is the story of Aurora,
A new dawn for the folk who bore her.
Her parents, who at ninety three,
Seem really rather old to me.

Her father, Jeremy, was King,
Not of a country, but a gypsy ring.
He was the eldest of the clan,
A very strong and able man.

His wife was barren all these years.
They both had shed a lot of tears.

At last he did a deal with God
To strengthen up his magic rod,
To give new life to Martha's womb
And make it fertile, not a tomb.

But in return his God insisted,
Something not to be resisted,
To send his concubine away,
Whose child would now be in the way.

They wandered through another land,
Which wasn't quite the life they'd planned.
Deprived of all inheritance,
They struggled to make any sense.

Maria told of small Aurora
And how her father did adore her.
Hearing this tale, the young Camilla
Swore she'd be the one to kill her.

She would avenge her mother's honour
And this Princess would be a goner.
She practiced on her gypsy curse,
To make it proof against reverse.

She learned to speak the words so loud
They would be heard above the crowd.
She learned to say the words so shrill
The very sound alone might kill.

And if you think this sounds too rotten,
And the curser misbegotten,
How would you feel, in life's race,
If someone else just stole your place?

Most of us have never cursed,
We cannot even speak in verse.
Only a few know how to pray
And never learn the words which slay.

"Sticks and stones may break my bones
But words will never harm me,"
Is just the thoughtless language,
That they teach you in the army.
But if you are believing this,
Some folk will think you're barmy.

I dare not write it down here,
The words of her foul curse.
But one thing I can tell you,
It was full of rhyming verse.

They all knew it was coming,
One big day of celebration.
The news, it spread like wildfire
All across the gypsy nation.

The heads of every family
Received an invitation.
They all joined in with praises
For God's marvelous creation.

And each of them brought blessings
For the baby's little head,
Til Camilla arrived
And filled them all with dread.

The curse was sworn.
She had it taped.
But worse than that,
The girl escaped!

There was no wise man to undo it
And sadly everybody knew it.
But there was one with a computer,
Who found on it a spell to suit her.
Though this could not undo the curse,
It could provide a kind of nurse
To keep her body out of death,
Surviving on a little breath.

Now this would be Aurora's fate,
The curse would start a little late.
She would become a child of beauty,
Grace and charm and even duty,

Until she reached her fifteenth year,
A date that filled them all with fear,
For this had been Camilla's age,
When banishment had made her rage.

The curse predicted that her fate
Was that she trusted in her mate,
And she would make her worse than sick,
By giving her a needle prick.

Her parents tried to stop the thing
Through council of the gypsy ring.
They ruled that all hard drugs should be
Expelled from their society.

Aurora grew through adolescence.
She never went out poaching pheasants.
But with her friend called Moriarty,
She loved to sneak off to a party.

Now, Moriarty was a girl,
Who lived outside the gypsy world.
T'was rumoured she was into drugs.
She thought Aurora's parents mugs.

One night, while playing party tricks,
She gave her friend a little fix.
Though just a little heroin,
And scarcely stronger than some gin,
It did our poor Aurora in.

Just like it's in Fellini's Roma,
Our girl has passed into a coma.
Soon, she's in a hospital bed.
The wicked Moriarty's fled.

Of course, her parents are distraught.
They're frozen up in word and thought,
And nothing that the doctors brought her
Helped revive their darling daughter.

Years and years and years went by
And there was not a single guy
Could make her give the slightest cry.

Though everyone was very kind,
They could not get inside her mind,
Fearing some terrors there to find.

One day a young psychiatrist
Found some strange pulse upon her wrist,
And there and then it seemed to him
That he must go out on a limb.

He'd go where he'd not been before,
Just like a soldier in a war.
He'd try a special new machine,
To go where none had ever been.

Although he feared he would be blind,
The pulse took him inside her mind.
He found himself inside her dreams.
His brain was bursting at the seams.

But still our hero ventured on
To reach where no man else had gone.
He found himself inside a thicket
And doubted whether he could stick it.

The thicket led inside a tunnel,
A very strange and wondrous funnel.
Eventually he reached the top
And this is where he had to stop.

Now he was in a castle keep,
Where sweet Aurora lay asleep.

To him she seemed so beautiful.
He knew he should be dutiful,
But Leo pondered long on this,
Could he just give her one small kiss?

At last he makes two Freudian slips,
He kisses her upon her lips.

Before his exit he can make,
Our heroine is wide awake.

Before his psyche's back in place,
Aurora slaps him round the face.
And now our young man's in a swoon,
His mind is swinging round the moon.

But lying there, he looks so pretty,
She feels a sudden burst of pity.
She takes his hand, and up he wakes,
Declaring that he'd dreamed of snakes.

Now very soon these two are wed
And legally in the same bed.
They feel so close in heart and mind.
No matter that their love was blind.

The moral of this tale is clear.
You can't escape the things you fear,
But if you struggle with your fate
You still may find a lovely mate.

JACK AND THE BEAN STALK

Get up, my son. We'll take a walk.
I'll tell of Jack's amazing stalk.

This isn't my imagination,
His stalk stretched out to every Nation.

His mother thought him not too bright,
But you will see she was not right.

Her husband, he had run away,
Escaping from the CSA.

She worked her larynx to the bone
By selling on the telephone.

Call centres do not pay that well.
Their basement flat began to smell.

Cos Jack would seldom go to school,
She thought he'd turn into a fool.

One day she said "I've had enough.
Its time to dump this smelly stuff.

Your room is filling up with junk
And you are smelling like a skunk.

This stuff is just beyond the pail.
Its going to a car boot sale.

I'll have to sell off my stuff too
To pay the rent that's overdue."

And so they loaded up the car.
They did not have to drive that far.

They have them every Sunday morn
Even the day that Christ was born!

A modern version of religion,
A place to even sell your fridge in.

The pitches stretched for miles and miles.
The goods set out in endless piles.

Not far from them a magic man
Unloaded things from his old van.

Though people said he was a spy,
To Jack he seemed a friendly guy.

He had some very special phones
That played the most enchanting tones.

One had the most amazing case.
It certainly was in yer face.

To own a mobile phone like this
Would be for, Jack, such total bliss,

That he would trade just everything,
Even his mother's wedding ring.

And Jack was such a cheeky kid
That was exactly what he did.

When mum came back from having tea,
The only thing left there to see

Was Jack and his computer phone.
It made her scream. It made her moan.

She beat him hard around the head
Till Jack was very nearly dead.

She threw the shiny phone away
So Jack could never with it play.

Then she and Jack went home to bed.
She put some plasters on his head.

But our hero not only survived his mum's rocket
He smuggled the super new phone in his pocket.

The morning came, he switched it on,
And suddenly our hero's gone.

He only has to punch a digit,
While being careful not to fidget.

He holds the case and the aerial stalk.
He doesn't even have to talk.

He finds he's in another land
With any place at his command.

He thinks the Bank of England's nice,
And finds he's got there in a trice.

The guards had guns and seemed in charge.
To Jack they looked immensely large.

But by and by they went to sleep,
And slowly forward Jack could creep.

He found himself inside the vault
With no one there to tell him halt.

Then he phoned home with lots of money.
Jack thought the whole thing rather funny.

Now even mum was rather pleased.
Their finance problems all were eased.

But soon young Jack was wanting more
And staying home was just a bore.

The phone stalk suddenly vibrated,
The destination calibrated.

Our Jack goes through the stratosphere.
He isn't even feeling queer.

He's broken into Microsoft
Bill Gates' very private loft.

To steal his new computer disc
Seemed worthy of the greatest risk.

Before his journey home he rings
The stolen disc to Bill Gates sings.
Our hero needs a red bull's wings.

As big Bill Gates comes after Jack
Its not a time for being slack.

Our hero, being far from thick,
Invents a plan that's very slick.

The two of them are in a race
Both travelling through cyberspace.

Before the audience can cough
Our hero turns the mobile off.

The ogre has not reached his station
So he goes into fragmentation.

Now Jack and mum are rich beyond measure.
They both devote their lives to pleasure.

Now son, there's messages in this tale.
Its still o.k. to be young and male.

Its possible to achieve your dream,
Just dodge computer discs that scream.

ROSIE AND HAL or THE ICE QUEEN

High up on all our horror lists
We put those crazy scientists,
The ones whose intellects aren't small,
But haven't any hearts at all.

Now, if we judge the ones who risk it,
The bloke who really takes the biscuit,
The man who made the whole world ill,
Is the physicist from Chernobyl.

We have to keep these folk in check
To save the world from total wreck.

Right through the skies the wind Gods hurled
Chernobyl dust around the world,
And if a drop fell in their eye,
Then any child began to cry.

No matter what the parents tried
The dust went festering inside.
But then it seemed to go away.
The children could go back to play.

The people all too soon forgot,
But later some wished that they'd not.
Which brings the start of this fine tale,
So listen well and do not fail.

Its all about a 'Queen of Ice',
A story of peculiar vice.
A very wicked queen was she,
As wicked as a queen can be.

Some say the ice queen's just a myth
Like Adam and Eve, or the demon, Lilith.
But she's as real as real can be,
As you will very quickly see.

Now let me introduce our heroes,
As academics, maybe zeros,
But learning happens outside schools
And our kids certainly aren't fools.

I met them in a shopping mall,
Two little kids, Rosie and Hal.

Hal was older, and a boy.
He was our Rosie's pride and joy.
Hal loved his little Rosie too.

Rosie was sure Hal wasn't mean.
Two smarter kids, I've never seen.

I promise you he loved her true.
They used to play the whole day through,
Except that day the dust clouds blew.

Rosie was kept all safe inside,
While Hal went out, on a cycle ride.
A dust spec landed in his eye.
There isn't any reason why.
But soon his life had gone awry.
His spirit had begun to die.

Leukemia, the doctors said,
The trouble wasn't in his head,
But in his blood. Those cells, once red,
Were dying, filling him with dread.

His cheeks, that once were shining bright,
Were slowly turning deathly white.
As colour faded from his face,
It turned to scowls and dark grimace.
He felt that life was so unfair,
That Rosie's smile was always there.
She loved him, but he did not care,
And if she came to him he'd swear,
And send her packing down the stair.

Poor Rosie couldn't understand
Why he rejected all they'd planned.
First he was stubborn as a mule,
But then he started getting cruel.

If she would hug him in the street
He'd try to knock her off her feet.
At school he'd pull her chair away
As she was sitting. What a cheat.
If Rose still trusted, he'd repeat,
Till all the hope in her seemed beat.

Then winter snows blew into town.
Young Hal was feeling very down.

But one day in the central square,
He thought he'd found the answer there.
Wrapped in a coat of dazzling white,
Her stethoscope, a shining light,
Her lips all glossed with magic ointment,
She offers Hal instant appointment.

Our modern ice queen is a doctor.
Rosie couldn't look, it shocked her.
They jumped up on her motor sleigh,
And Rosie watched them ride away.

To Hal she offered wondrous cure.
To Rose it seemed a vicious lure.
This doctor had a heart of ice.
Rosie could tell she was not nice.

The hook was barbed, the line was cast
The ice queen held her victim fast.
As Rosie walked back home that day
The ice queen drove Hal far away.

Till now his treatment was a mess,
Just waiting for the N.H.S.
This was a very special deal
With funding from a cancer appeal.

Hal was very keen to go,
But where he went he did not know.
The doctor took a lengthy history,
But the hospital remained a mystery.

Rosie deeply loved her friend.
It nearly drove her round the bend,
Not knowing where poor Hal was sent,
Or if this doctor might be bent.

Then finally, in desperation,
And guided by imagination,
She set off in her friend's pursuit.
All wrapped in furs, she did look cute.

"I say there, can you help at all.
I'm looking for a hospital,"
She called to everyone she met.
Her plans were very clearly set.

The days went by. She walked and walked.
To every traveller she talked.
But none had even heard of Hal.
"Go home," they said, "you silly Gal."

She vowed she'd not admit defeat,
Though frostbite nibbled at her feet.
She sometimes slept in hospital basements,
Not exactly children's placements,
But at least each space was kind-of warm,
A refuge from the winter storm.

Then one day as she walked along,
Trying to sing a happy song,
A gang of street kids spotted her
And tore away her coat of fur.
They would have stabbed her with a knife
Had not the leader saved her life.

He said "I really fancy you,
And this is what you've got to do.
Join our gang and help us rob.
We'll give you food to fill your gob."

But Rose was having none of it.
She called the boy a silly tit.
He said, "If you won't join our gang
Then I'm afraid you'll have to hang."

They hung poor Rosie by her toes.
How she endured it no one knows,
Especially when they stole her clothes.

The little street boy so admired
The energy with which she's fired,
He cut her down,
Gave her a gown,
And said that she deserved his crown.

But Rose just wanted to go on
To find that place where Hal had gone.
He lent to her his favourite dog,
With skills to guide her on her slog.

Then she set off with heartfelt thanks,
Along the ancient river banks.
Rose climbed upon the dogs' great back,
His nose sniffed out the ice queen's track,

And very soon they reached the place.
'Twas just like being in a race.
The dog then stopped, and said goodbye.
To go in here he would not try.
She gave her friend a great big bone
And boldly ventured in alone.

The hospital was huge and white
And lit with every kind of light.
But something surely was not right.
She knew that she would have to fight.

Now Rosie started feeling old.
The atmosphere turned very cold.
And any staff she met would scold.
But she would simply not be told.

Now doctors really do need science,
But they need more than just compliance,
To form a medical alliance.
They have to stay in touch with feelings,
If they're to achieve some real healings.

The ice queen started off all right,
Before descending into night.
Faced with so much human harm,
She stuck a needle in her arm.
Then, with her human feelings cut off,
She found that she could work her butt off.

But when she finally reached the top
She really did not want to stop.
A cold ambition drove her higher,
Made her worse than just a lier.

She was the queen of all research.
They worshiped her like God in church.
The heroin inside her veins
Helped her keep hold of all the reins.
She needed lots of boys like Hal
To keep her living in Pall Mall.

Her treatments became very cruel,
But no one dared contest her rule.
To do so you'd be thought a fool.

Faced with so much human pain,
They thought the only way to gain
Was shutting out the smallest shiver,
See not a person, just a liver.

"The spleen in bed no. thirty three
Is looking pretty good to me."
Is how the doctors all would talk,
As down the corridors they'd walk.

Hal was turning very pale.
You'd hardly guess that he was male.
He learned to cut off any feeling
And disappear up to the ceiling.

The science could not work alone.
He needed love from folks at home.
And only Rose could give him this,
A very special loving kiss.

She met the ice queen's fierce ambition
With her own female intuition.
She guessed the woman's use of a drug,
And quickly pulled away the rug,
Exposing all her drug supply,
Telling the world the reasons why.

The ice queen's rule melted away
And Hal got stronger every day.
His cells grew red. His heart grew warm.
The children had survived their storm.

And finally the pair went home.
They promised never more to roam,
Without at least a fond goodbye,
And sharing all the reasons why.

So when you're working in your study,
And human weakness seems too bloody,
Know that the heart too has its reasons.
It leads you through your winter seasons.

GOLDILOCKS

This is a tale that isn't fair,
The story of the family Bear.

I don't know why we call them Bear,
Maybe they had a lot of hair.
Perhaps they all were naturists,
With great big teeth and great big fists.

They are a group of only three,
There's mum and dad and big "baby".
Why he's called "baby" I'm not sure,
Perhaps because they think he's pure!

The truth is that he's growing up,
Almost too old to be still a pup,

But Goldilocks is even bigger,
When she jumps in, like Pooh's friend Tigger.

Some call this story Goldilocks,
'Cos its about the day she knocks
Upon their door,
Checking the score.
"There's no one in - oh, what a bore."

The Bears have gone out for a ride,
So Goldilocks can slip inside.

They've left the porridge cooling down.
The steaming bowls make Goldie frown.

There should be several people here.
Where have they gone? It seems so queer.
The hunger gnaws at Goldilocks,
Her inhibitions it unblocks.

Now please don't think that Goldy's frumpy,
She just finds daddy's porridge lumpy.
Mummy's has got too much salt.
It needs some sugar or some malt.

The smallest bowl, it tastes so good.
She scoffs it down - you knew she would.

Then Goldy tries out all the chairs.
They're all in need of some repairs.

The daddy's chair is much too hard,
Far better left out in the yard.

And mummy's chair is much too tall.
She can't get comfy there at all.

Though baby's chair is not that small,
It breaks beneath her, and she falls.

Poor Goldy bangs her pretty head.
She thinks she needs to lie in bed.

Then daddy's bed is much too high.
This cannot be the one to try.

And mummy's bed is much too lumpy.
Goldy can't sleep there, it's bumpy.

But baby's bed feels rather nice.
She falls asleep there in a trice.

The Bears return to eat their food.
Their ride has put them in the mood.

The empty bowl causes dismay.
"Who could have eaten it?" they say.

And then they spot the baby's chair.
It's broken; but there's no one there!

Before you even turn this page
The Bears have flown into a rage.

In anger they all charge about.
Where is the thief? They'll soon find out.

The baby charges up the stair.
He thinks he'll find the answer there.

He rushes straight into his room,
His face all red like its in bloom.

But Goldy's face appears so pretty,
The little bear is moved to pity.

He thinks at once that she should stay,
But Goldy wakes and runs away.
The bear's red face near turns her grey.
Oh, what a dreadful place to play.

She crashes through the window pain.
He fears his first love's all in vain.

Poor Goldy lands on broken glass.
There's one bit sticking in her ass.

With blood all dripping from her rear,
She does not want to hang round here.

She disappears into the wood.
I guess you always knew she would.

Our little bear is broken hearted.
He's much worse off than when he started.

He's lost a friend with whom to play.
It's horrid that she would not stay.
But crossness had got in his way.

Is there a moral to this tale?
There's many try, they mostly fail.

We try to find where we belong.
Sometimes we simply get it wrong.

To some we're big, to some we're small
Sometimes we don't fit in at all.

SNOW WHITE

You've heard the story of Snow White
And maybe you just thought it trite.
Another wicked step-mama,
Who kills as freely as a Czar.

But listen and you soon will see,
She's really more like you and me.
A woman, young, and just a bride,
Finds Snow White growing deep inside.

Perhaps you'll call it a displacement,
Concealing Snow White in this basement.
But I will have to disagree,
For this is how it looks to me.

It's fairy tales that do displace,
To stop our mother's losing face.
Our images of mum we split,
Protecting from the nasty bit.

Our mums preserved at any price
From qualities that aren't too nice.
In stories it's so often said,
the heroes real mum is dead.

Good mum's preserved from all decay.
Now she is safely out the way,
The child can keep her as ideal,
A happier way for her to feel.

Then step-mother can be so black
There won't be any fault she'll lack.

My version is not just a game
And I shall have to take the blame
For telling the unpleasant truth
About a woman's loss of youth.

Now Mary was a pretty girl,
Who loved her teenage social whirl.
Perhaps, she really should have tarried,
Instead of which she soon got married.

But marrying was not a flop.
He was the pick of all the crop.
For he had money in the bank,
And muscles bulging like a tank.

He had the handsomest of faces
And contacts in the highest places.
The man was a terrific catch.
It really seemed the smartest match.

Now Jim was nearly thirty three,
But supple as a willow tree.
He liked his women rather younger,
To keep him virile, make him stronger.

He worked at night, a disco jockey,
And at week-ends he loved his hockey.
He could have several girls a night,
With never a thought it wasn't right.

But Mary thought that he would change,
Now he'd explored the widest range.
And he fell so in love with Mary,
That he'd forgotten to be wary.

Their marriage happened very fast,
The sort of thing that doesn't last.
But soon our Mary's in the club,
Something that made her blub and blub.

Her husband did not have to rape her
To change the colored litmus paper.
She was changing to a different pill.
The other one had made her ill.

The sperm and egg met in the break,
A very lucky chance to take.
She was as fertile as could be,
So very full of health was she.

The father's utterly delighted,
But Mary fears her youth is blighted.
She's certain that it's just her beauty
That keeps her man doing his duty.

If she's no more with beauty graced,
She fears that she will be replaced,
As closest to her man's faint heart,
And soon the two will fall apart.

She's terrified to lose her figure.
Inevitably she'll get bigger.
And once she's lost her perfect features,
He's sure to sleep with other creatures.

Mary has scarce outgrown her mum.
Now there's a baby in her tum.
She is sure it isn't fair
To have to keep that baby there.

The future of this babe she'll block.
She pays a visit to the doc.
"Now, doctor, you must clearly see
You should dispose of this for me."

The doc, because of his religion
Refuses her this big decision,
Says she should be a duteous wife,
"It's very wrong to take a life."

She hurries home feeling so mad,
The doctor should have called her bad.

She feels a flutter in her womb.
She'd hoped it was the baby's tomb.
But now she knows the baby's there,
But still this mother does not care.

She's drained by this strange alien
And fears her beauty may be gone.
Says "Mirror, mirror, on my wall,
Am I still fairer than them all?"

Now mirrors cannot answer back.
This is a talent that they lack.
But all psychology has said,
We've different voices in our head.

It's one of these that answers back,
"There isn't anything you lack.
But as this baby's growing bigger
Then you are sure to lose your figure,
And even if Jim does not leave,
Then soon it will be time to grieve.
For one thing I can tell you true,
This babe is prettier than you.
He will prefer his new-born child,
And this is going to drive you wild."

How did she know this was the truth?
And was she a deluded youth?
Her dad preferred her to her mum,
So she was sure her time was come.

Now every year since Oedipus,
Parents have made a lot of fuss,
Not that their children will disgrace 'em,
But rather that they will displace them.

The father, frightened of his son,
Retaliates, as life's begun.
I don't care if you chose to scoff,
Thats why he cuts the foreskin off.

This is a warning of castration
To sons who get above their station.

And daughters can replace their mother,
In turning Dad into their lover.
Of course this is in fantasy,
And all a matter of degree.

Our Mary was no mother mild.
She felt so threatened by her child.
Her life has scarce become her own.
Too soon for turning to a crone.

With children, you're no longer free.
With this you will not disagree.
The virgin state is gone for good,
When women enter motherhood.

A virgin is not simply green.
Before sex, isn't what I mean.
It is an independent state,
A woman free and feeling great.

The baby is a strange intruder.
(I know I could have put it cruder).

Mary decides it's got to go,
Before the thing begins to grow.

A knitting needle granny brings;
So useful for these sort of things.
The violence, done with one quick jerk,
Fails to achieve its deadly work.

But deep inside the young Snow White
Is feeling very far from right.

Her body did at least survive.
It doesn't mean that she can thrive.
The trauma damages her mind.
This action, which is so unkind.

Her psyche into pieces splits.
No longer whole, she's all in bits.

The womb, no longer her safe place,
the cradle of the human race.
It's turned into a deep, dark wood,
Somewhere that's anything but good.

Umbilicus becomes a mine.
Resources needed all the time.
She's fearful of her mum's attack.
Her future's looking very black.

She splits to dwarf-selves numbered seven,
Who build for her a phony heaven.
Her main self's hiding in her head,
Doing its best to fend off dread.

Sleepy, Grumpy and the rest,
Work very hard to do their best.
Desperately, they rush about,
Trying to keep her mother out.

They're mining her umbilicus,
Trying not to make a fuss.
Pumping water out the mine,
Keeps them busy all the time.

But having all these helpful boys in
Can't keep out the mother's poison.
There is not a single chap'll
Stop her eating mother's apple.

Mother's now enormous girth
Ensures that she must now give birth.
To keep herself from labour pains
Pethidine goes through her veins.

For babe, this is an overdose,
So she starts turning comatose.
And to the doctor's great dismay
The baby starts to fade away.

The womb may yet become her coffin
Without the help of some great boffin.
With forceps placed around her head
The babe emerges on the bed.

But there is still a lot to do.
Poor Snow White's turned three shades of blue.
The tale describes a great glass casket.
Our girl might have preferred a basket.

They put her in an incubator,
For she'll revive sooner or later.
Then daddy comes upon the scene.
Seeing her blue, it turns him green.

He picks her up, gives her a kiss.
A wonderful relief this is.
The baby very slowly wakes,
And bonding with her father makes.

His girl becomes his fond obsession,
While mum gets peurperal depression.

I've told a tale you thought you knew,
And now you've heard the one thats true.

Applications

The poems are there for all to enjoy.

But for those who also see them as stepping-stones to greater understanding, or as a tool in their working lives, the second section of the book introduces a choice of applications for the work.

They can be made use of in a number of different fields. We have identified four for your consideration.

Personal development

Managemnent development

Schools and Colleges

Youth Work

For more information, dates, times and venues email info@trans-itions.com or visit www.trans-itions.com

Application 1

Personal development

"Waking from enchantment"

A two day workshop designed to open up the truth of personal and familial relationships through the exploration of fairy tales.

The patterns of the past can be like the ground during winter, a frozen crust several feet thick. The enactment of a fairy tale can bring the patterns, like green shoots, out into the light of day, where they can be examined, understood and transformed.

The structure of the workshop will be experiential, with a focus on learning by enactment and analysis.

People can expect to make discoveries about their personal history, including relationships with parents and siblings. They will also discover and explore connections with other members of the group which will be mutually illuminating.

The workshop will lead the way to making new life choices and life changes.

For more information, dates, times and venues email info@trans-itions.com or visit www.trans-itions.com

Application 2

Management: Team Development

A better performance

If you really want to know what is going on in your team, then this course is what you are looking for.

Team members are given all kinds of roles in the collective goal of getting the job done well. But there are lots of other roles that come into the picture, without anyone intending to create them. King, Ogre, Victim, Hero, Dumbling, Heroine, Mentor, Guardian, Witch, and Trickster are but a few of the characters that appear in your team work unannounced. They are not all working for a happy-ever-after ending! They can cost your company dearly if allowed to go about their work out of awareness.

These roles have been around for hundreds of years in fairytales. For thirty years Nick Owen has been researching how fairytale characters affect our working together in groups. His forthcoming book, "Journeys to integration" describes how it works.

With the development of awareness, even the most terrible ogre can become a hero and a valuable team member. Nick's courses use the enactment of fairytale material to bring team dynamics to light and point the way to effective solutions. The courses are intense, powerful, demanding and a lot of fun.

Format 1   Residential, two days, with on-site follow up.

Format 2   One day, non-residential, with on-site follow up.

Format 3   Tailor-made, for on-site requirements.

When to use these courses?

1) At the start of a team's life to establish good working relationships between team members. It is an incredibly powerful way of getting to know people and how they relate to you.

2) When things are not working well and diagnosis and remedy of problems are needed. The enactment will unerringly go to the heart of the matter.

3) As a resourcing balance to stressful task-oriented team work. It is important to know the "how " of what you are doing as well as the "what".

4) As a celebration of the completion of a successful piece of work. The work is deep, but it is also tremendous fun and liberating in a way that only drama can be.

For more information, dates, times and venues email info@trans-itions.com or visit www.trans-itions.com

Application 3

Schools and Colleges

Nick Owen is available to provide readings and talks about the poetry to student groups in colleges, primary and secondary schools.

Trans-itions is able to help further with creative exploration of the themes in the poems by supplying schemes of work for schools at Key Stage 3 and Key Stage 4 in the National Curriculum.

Children can use the poems in the subject areas of;
English,
Drama,
PSHE.

Course work will involve reading, writing, speaking, listening, discussion and drama in relation to adolescent experience.

Teacher's packs will provide staff with tools to satisfy National Curriculum requirements.

For more information, dates, times and venues email info@trans-itions.com or visit www.trans-itions.com

Application 4

Social Care

Social Services, Youth Departments and Voluntary Agencies may find that they can use the poetry from this book in their care work.

Trans-itions offers courses that will be tailored to the needs of a particular organisation.

Possible applications include:

1) Training for care staff in using fairytales with client groups

2) Using fairytale material as a focus for staff team study days

3) Events at conferences

For more information, dates, times and venues email info@trans-itions.com or visit www.trans-itions.com

About the author

Nick Owen was born in Bromsgrove in 1950. His father, a local politician, brought new life to medaieval festivals and rituals in the town, so that Nick grew up with a strong sense of ritual and story. His poetic talents first appeared printed in the Malvernian journal while he was at school. At Keele University he graduated in Psychology and Philosophy and directed plays, going on to qualify as a Drama teacher in 1974.

Nick taught in London from 1974-1976, while studying Drama therapy and counselling.
After a period of social work with the Community Drug Project in Camberwell, he went into private practice as a counsellor. He began to lead fairytale focused personal development workshops at Playspace, Westminster Pastoral Foundation and Middlesex Polytechnic. He became one of the first graduates of the Institute of Pastoral Education and Counselling in 1980. There he became a member of the Board and National Training Committee, introducing Art and Drama work into the curriculum.

Nick worked in London Social Services as groupwork development and training officer for children and mental health services from 1980 to 1986. From 1986-7 he was an AIDS/HIV co-ordinator in the NHS.

In 1990 he founded the Oxford School of Psychotherapy and Counselling with Mary Duhig. The study of fairytales became a core part of the curriculum for students, many of whom went on to take part in the "Self and Others research project" exploring fairytales in personal history and peer relationships.

From 1998 Nick has worked intensively with people's birth and prebirth stories, setting up the Oxford Prenatal and Perinatal Education Research and Awareness trust.

Nick's work has always been focused on the drama of family life. He has worked in some of the most intense and demanding fields of social work, education and therapy. He now spends most of his time in personal and educational development work, social research, and writing plays and poetry. He has two daughters and two step sons.

About the illustrator

Adam Hinton was born in Barnsley in South Yorkshire in 1979. Adam drew Disney-like cartoons from the age of six. Art, drama and creative work excited him at school. He decided to specialise in graphic design, taking an HND in Northampton. Adam has worked at Windrush, as a designer for the last three years, and is developing his portfolio of illustrations. He lives in Thame with his partner.

Printed by

windrush
design · print · communications

windrush house, avenue two
station lane, witney
oxfordshire ox28 4xw

t 01993 772197
f 01993 771709
e info@windrushgroup.co.uk
w www.windrushgroup.co.uk

By the same author

The search for the beloved

The shaman and the psychotherapist

Collected poetry

Framing psychotherapy

More Gold into lead

The relationship

The vagina dualogues